Matters

Birdtober 2022

HAIKU

AN ANTHOLOGY
OF JAPANESE POEMS

Stephen Addiss, Fumiko Yamamoto,
and Akira Yamamoto

SHAMBHALA
Boston & London
2009

FRONTISPIECE: *Stream,* Tachibana Morikuni

SHAMBHALA PUBLICATIONS, INC.
Horticultural Hall
300 Massachusetts Avenue
Boston, Massachusetts 02115
www.shambhala.com

9   8   7   6   5   4   3   2

PRINTED IN CHINA

♻This edition is printed on acid-free paper that meets the
American National Standards Institute z39.48 Standard.
♻Shambhala Publications makes every effort to print on recycled paper.
For more information please visit www.shambhala.com.
Distributed in the United States by Random House, Inc.,
and in Canada by Random House of Canada Ltd

Library of Congress Cataloging-in-Publication Data
Haiku: an anthology of Japanese poems / [edited by] Stephen
Addiss, Fumiko Yamamoto, and Akira Yamamoto.—1st ed.
p.   cm.
ISBN 978-1-59030-730-4 (acid-free paper)
1. Haiku—Translations into English. I. Addiss, Stephen, 1935–
II. Yamamoto, Fumiko Y. III. Yamamoto, Akira Y.
PL782.E3H236 2009
895.6'104108—dc22
2009010381

CONTENTS

INTRODUCTION

HAIKU are now one of the best-known and most practiced forms of poetry in the world. Simple enough to be taught to children, they can also reward a lifetime of study and pursuit. With their evocative explorations of life and nature, they can also exhibit a delightful sense of playfulness and humor.

Called *haikai* until the twentieth century, haiku are usually defined as poems of 5-7-5 syllables with seasonal references. This definition is generally true of Japanese haiku before 1900, but it is less true since then with the development of experimental free-verse haiku and those without reference to season: for example, the poems of Santōka (1882–1940), who was well known for his terse and powerful free verse. Seasonal reference has also been less strict in *senryū,* a comic counterpart of haiku in which human affairs become the focus.

Freedom from syllabic restrictions is especially true for contemporary haiku composed in other languages. The changes are not surprising. English, for example, has a different rhythm from Japanese: English is "stress-timed" and Japanese "syllable-timed." Thus, the same content can be said in fewer syllables in English. Take, for example, the most famous of all haiku, a verse by Bashō (1644–94):

> Furu ike ya
> kawazu tobikomu
> mizu no oto

Furu means "old," *ike* means "pond or ponds," and *ya* is an exclamatory particle, something like "ah." *Kawazu* is a "frog or frogs"; *tobikomu,* "jump in"; *mizu,* "water"; *no,* the genitive "of"; and *oto,* "sound or sounds" (Japanese does not usually distinguish singular from plural). If using the singular, a literal translation would be:

> Old pond—
> a frog jumps in
> the sound of water

Only the third of these lines matches the 5-7-5 formula, and the other lines would require "padding" to fit the usual definition:

> [There is an] old pond—
> [suddenly] a frog jumps in
> the sound of water

This kind of "padding" tends to destroy the rhythm, simplicity, and clarity of haiku, so translations of 5-7-5–syllable Japanese poems are generally rendered with fewer syllables in English. Translators also have to choose whether to use singulars or plurals (such as *frog* or *frogs,* *pond* or *ponds,* and *sound* or *sounds*), while in Japanese these distinctions are nicely indeterminate.

We have attempted to offer English translation as close to the Japanese original as possible, line-by-line. Sometimes a parallel English translation succeeds in conveying the sense of the original. This haiku by Issa provides an example:

Japanese

> kasumu hi no *(mist day of)*
> uwasa-suru yara *(gossip-do maybe)*
> nobe no uma *(field of horse)*

Close Translation

> Misty day—
> they might be gossiping,
> horses in the field

Sometimes the attempt at a parallel translation results in awkward English, and a freer translation is necessary, as with this haiku by Buson:

Japanese

> yoru no ran *(night of orchid)*
> ka ni kakurete ya *(scent in hide wonder)*
> hana shiroshi *(flower be=white)*

Close Translation

> Evening orchid—
> is it hidden in its scent?
>   the white of its flower

Freer Translation

> Evening orchid—
> the white of its flower
>   hidden in its scent

Other times a parallel translation doesn't have the impact that can be delivered in a freer translation, as in this haiku by an anonymous poet:

Japanese

> mayoi-go no *(lost-child of)*
> ono ga taiko de *(one's=own drum with)*
>   tazunerare *(be=searched=for)*

Close Translation

> The lost child
> with his own drum
>   is searched for

Freer Translation

> Searching for
> the lost child
>   with his own drum

Thus, the challenge for translators is to try to follow the Japanese word and line order without resulting in awkward English. While admirable, sometimes adhering to the original verses may make for weaker poems in English. Sometimes the languages are too different to make a close match without hurting the flow and even the meaning. However, when closer translations succeed, they are powerfully satisfying.

The fact that the spirit of the haiku can be effectively rendered in English translation indicates that the 5-7-5 syllabic count captures the outward rhythmic form of traditional Japanese haiku but does not necessarily define them. The strength of haiku is their ability to suggest and evoke rather than merely to describe. With or without the 5-7-5 formula and seasonal references, readers are invited to place themselves in a poetic mode and to explore nature as their imaginations permit.

Returning to Bashō's frog, what does the poem actually say? On the surface, not very much—one or more frogs jumping into one or more ponds and making one or more sounds. Yet this poem has fascinated people for more than three hundred years, and the reason why remains something of a mystery. Is it that it combines old (the pond) and new (the jumping)? A long time span and immediacy? Sight and sound? Serenity and the surprise of breaking it? Our ability to harmonize with the nature? All of these may evoke an experience that we can share in our own imaginations.

Whatever meanings it brings forth in readers, this haiku has not only been appreciated but also variously modeled after and sometimes even parodied in Japan, the latter suggesting that readers should not take it too seriously. To give a few examples, the Chinese-style poet-painter Kameda Bōsai (1752–1826) wrote:

> Old pond—
> after that time
> no frog jumps in

while the Zen master Sengai Gibon (1750–1837) added new versions:

> Old pond—
> something has PLOP
> just jumped in

> Old pond—
> Bashō jumps in
> the sound of water

Bashō has become so famous for his haiku that this eighteenth-century *senryū* mocks the now self-conscious master himself:

> Master Bashō,
> at every plop
> stops walking

In the modern world, new transformations of this poem keep appearing even across the ocean, including this haiku with an environmental undertone by Stephen Addiss:

> Old pond paved over
> into a parking lot—
> one frog still singing

Perhaps one reason why haiku have become internationally popular in recent decades comes from our sensitivity to our surroundings, even to the development of towns and cities, often to the detriment of the natural world: poets have power to keep on singing the connection to nature in their new milieu.

Haiku in Japan

Although haiku is now a worldwide phenomenon, its roots stretch far back into Japan's history. The form itself began with poets sharing the composition of "linked verse" in the form of a series of five-line *waka* (5-7-5-7-7 syllables), a much older form of poem. *Waka* poets, working in sequence, noted that the 5-7-5–syllable sections could often stand alone. Separate couplets of 7-7 syllables were less appealing to the Japanese taste for asymmetry, but from the 5-7-5 links, haiku were born.

It is generally considered that Bashō was the poet

who brought haiku into full flowering, deepening and enriching it and also utilizing haiku in accounts of his travels such as *Oku no hosomichi* (Narrow Road to the Interior). Bashō's pupils then continued his tradition of infusing seemingly simple haiku with evocative undertones, while continuing a sense of play that kept haiku from becoming the least bit ponderous.

The next two of the "three great masters" were Buson (1716–83), a major painter as well as poet who developed haiku-painting (*haiga*) to its height, and Issa (1763–1827), whose profound empathy with all living beings was a major feature of his poetry. With the abrupt advent of Western civilization to Japan in the late nineteenth century, haiku seemed to be facing an uncertain future, but it was revived by Masaoka Shiki (1867–1902) and his followers, and it has continued unabated until the present day.

Despite some historical changes over the centuries, certain features of Japanese life and thought have maintained themselves as integral features of the haiku spirit. For example, the native religion of Shintō reveres deities in nature, both a cause and an effect of the Japanese love of trees, rocks, mountains, valleys, waterfalls, flowers, moss, animals, birds, insects, and so many more elements of the natural world. Significantly, haiku include human nature as an organic part in all of nature, as in the following poems about dragonflies by Shirao (1738–91) and the aforementioned Santōka, respectively:

The coming of autumn
is determined
by a red dragonfly

Dragonfly on a rock—
absorbed in
a daydream

In each case, the observation of an insect leads to a deeper consideration of our own perceptions, although neither poem has a "moral" or an obvious message. We may well ask who is judging, and who is daydreaming? In this sense, it could be said that every haiku is at least partially about human beings, if only the one who originally composed it and the one reading and experiencing it now. Perhaps all fine poems are expressions of experience rather than merely "things," and haiku, above all, elicit our own participation as readers, almost as though the poet had disappeared and left us to determine our own experience.

There has been some controversy about the influence of Zen in haiku. Certainly some poets (such as Bashō) studied Zen, and a few were actually Zen masters (such as Sengai). Many other Japanese poets, however, followed other Buddhist sects, Shintō, or were completely secular, so we should be careful about claiming too much direct influence of Zen. In a broader sense, however, Japanese culture and the arts during the past seven centuries have been suffused with Zen influence, ranging from the tea ceremony and flower arranging to Noh theater, ink painting, and *shakuhachi* (bamboo flute) music. In particular, Zen's insistence on the enlightenment of the ordinary world at the present moment, right here and right now, has both mirrored and influenced the haiku spirit. As Issa wrote:

> Where there are people
> there are flies, and
> there are Buddhas

The Zen influence in haiku may need more examination, but it has touched Japanese culture so deeply that it can never be entirely absent. What Zen, other Buddhist sects, and Shintō all have in common with haiku is the harmony between nature and humans.

Regarding This Volume

The three author-editors of the present volume have previously published a series of five books: *A Haiku Menagerie* (Weatherhill, 1992), *A Haiku Garden* (Weatherhill, 1996), *Haiku People* (Weatherhill, 1998), *Haiku Landscapes* (Weatherhill, 2002), and *Haiku Humor* (Weatherhill, 2007). The haiku in this new book are excerpted from those books, with some modifications in translation, along with newly added verses. This anthology includes a representative number of poems by each of the three great masters (Bashō, Buson, and Issa), a generous group of haiku by observant and creative poets ranging in time from the early fifteenth through the later twentieth centuries, and a sprinkling of anonymous comical *senryū*.

The poems are grouped into three categories: The Pulse of Nature, Human Voices, and Resonance and Reverberation. Each category moves along a time line, not linearly but rather cyclically, reflecting natural life rhythms.

These poems are expressions not only of Japanese sensibilities but of age-old human responses to the world around us. We wish all of our readers the joy of experiencing this kaleidoscope of all living creatures and their multifaceted interactions with enveloping nature as expressed by the finest Japanese haiku and *senryū* poets.

The Pulse of Nature

Opening their hearts
ice and water become
friends again

— TEISHITSU

The spring sun
shows its power
between snowfalls

— SHIGEYORI

Not in a hurry
to blossom—
plum tree at my gate

— ISSA

White plum blossoms
return to the withered tree—
moonlit night

— BUSON

The warbler
wipes its muddy feet
on plum blossoms

— ISSA

With each falling petal
they grow older—
plum branches

—Buson

Dried grasses—
and just a few heat waves
rising an inch or two

—Bashō

Overflowing with love
the cat as coquettish
as a courtesan

— SAIMARO

Both partners
sport whiskers—
cats' love

— RAIZAN

Spring sun
in every pool of water—
lingering

— ISSA

Is the dawn, too,
still embraced by
hazy moon?

—CHŌSUI

In the shimmering haze
the cat mumbles something
in its sleep

—ISSA

Spring rain—
just enough to wet tiny shells
on the tiny beach

—BUSON

The nurseryman
left behind
   a butterfly

— RYŌTA

Again and again
stitching the rows of barley—
   a butterfly

— SORA

A pheasant's tail
very gently brushes
the violets
— SHŪSHIKI-JO

Over the violets
a small breeze
passes by
— ONTEI

Each time the wind blows
the butterfly sits anew
on the willow
— BASHŌ

Spring chill—
above the rice paddies
rootless clouds
— HEKIGODŌ

Daybreak—
the whitefish whiten
only one inch
— BASHŌ

Domestic ducks
stretch their necks
hoping to see the world
— KŌJI

The warbler
dropped his hat—
a camellia

— BASHŌ

Crazed by flowers
surprised by the moon—
a butterfly

— CHORA

White camellias—
only the sound of their falling
moonlit night

— RANKŌ

Squeaking in response
to baby sparrows—
a nest of mice

— BASHŌ

Out from the darkness
back into the darkness—
affairs of the cat

—ISSA

Joyful at night
tranquil during the day—
spring rain

—CHORA

A camellia falls
spilling out
yesterday's rain

—BUSON

A hedge of thorns—
how skillfully the dog
　wriggled under it!

—Issa

Misty day—
they might be gossiping
　horses in the field

—Issa

An old well—
falling into its darkness
a camellia

—BUSON

Trampling on clouds,
inhaling the mist,
the skylark soars

—SHIKI

Crouching,
studying the clouds—
a frog

—CHIYO-JO

On the temple bell
perching and sleeping—
a butterfly

—BUSON

Could they be sutras?
in the temple well
frogs chant

—KANSETSU

Recited on and on,
the poems of the frogs
have too many syllables

— Eiji

Bracing his feet
and offering up a song—
the frog

— Sōkan

From the nostril
of the Great Buddha comes
a swallow

— Issa

On the brushwood gate
in place of a lock—
one snail

—ISSA

Sunlight
passes through a butterfly
asleep

—RANKŌ

With the power of non-attachment
floating on the water—
   a frog

                — Jōsō

Highlighting the blossoms,
clouded by blossoms—
   the moon

                — Chora

Flower petals
set the mountain in motion—
   cherry blossoms

                — Hōitsu

On the surface
of petal-covered water—
frogs' eyes

— FŪSEI

The retreating shapes
of the passing spring—
wisteria

— KANA-JO

Spring passes—
the last reluctant
cherry blossoms

— BUSON

Shallow river
twisting west and twisting east—
young leaves

— BUSON

Forsythia—
and radiant spring's
melancholy

— MANTARŌ

In daytime "darken the day"
at night "brighten the night"
frogs chant

—BUSON

Crossing the sea
into a net of mist—
the setting sun

—BUSON

Misty grasses—
water without voices
in the dusk

—BUSON

Spring passing—
looking at the sea,
a baby crow

—SHOKYŪ

The cuckoo
with a single song
has established summer

—RYŌTA

The voice of the cuckoo
slants
over the water

—BASHŌ

The cuckoo calls—
and the waters of the lake
cloud over a little

—Jōsō

The cuckoo—
flies and insects,
listen well!

—Issa

Summer rains—
leaves of the plum
the color of cold wind
— SAIMARO

Early summer rains—
lunging at the blue sea
muddy waters
— BUSON

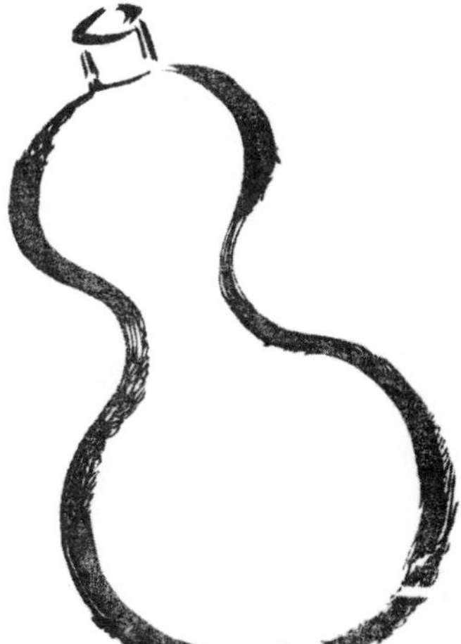

Early summer rains—
even nameless rivers
are fearsome

—BUSON

Summer cool—
in the green rice fields
a single pine

—SHIKI

Only Fuji
remains unburied—
young leaves

—BUSON

On the hydrangeas
the weight of the morning sun,
the evening sun

— OTSUYŪ

Mountain ant—
seen so clearly
on the white peony

— BUSON

Alone, silently—
the bamboo shoot
    becomes a bamboo
                — SANTŌKA

The warbler
amid the bamboo shoots
    sings of old age
                — BASHŌ

A triangle—
is the lizard's head getting
a little longer?

— KYOSHI

In my dwelling
friendly with the mice—
fireflies

— ISSA

How interesting—
running errands right and left
fireflies

— KAIGA

Pursued,
it hides in the moon—
the firefly

— SANO RYŌTA

Burning so easily,
extinguishing so easily—
the firefly

— CHINE-JO

The morning breeze
ripples the fur
of the caterpillar

— BUSON

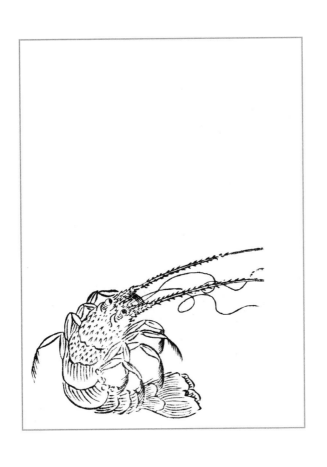

As the lake breeze
cools his bottom
the cicada cries

—Issa

As lightning flashes
he strokes his head—
the toad

—Issa

The snake flees—
but the eyes that peered at me
remain in the weeds
— KYOSHI

Rustling, rustling,
the lotus leaves sway—
a tortoise in the pond
— ONITSURA

Today too
mosquito larvae—
and tomorrow again
— ISSA

As flies retreat
mosquitoes start
their battle cry
—Anonymous

Dashing into one another
whispering, parting—
ants
—Anonymous

Inhaling clouds
exhaling clouds—
mountaintop pines
—Anonymous

Across a pillar of mosquitoes
hangs the bridge
of dreams

— KIKAKU

Even the clams
keep their mouths shut
in this heat

— BASHŌ

Motionless
in a crevice of an old wall—
a pregnant spider

—SHIKI

Heat in waves—
in the stones
angry reverberations

—KYŌTAI

Sudden shower—
and rising from the heat,
the broken-down horse

—KITŌ

Lightning!
fleeing up the wall,
the legs of a spider
— KICHŌ

Sudden shower—
clutching the blades of grass
a flock of sparrows
— BUSON

Down a paulownia tree
the rain comes trickling
across a cicada's belly
— BAISHITSU

The tree frog
riding the plantain leaf
    sways

— KIKAKU

"It's much too long a day,"
opening its mouth
    a crow

— ISSA

The fish
not knowing they're in a bucket
cool by the gate
—Issa

A sudden shower
drums down upon
the heads of the carp
—Shiki

Lightning—
yesterday to the east
today to the west
— KIKAKU

Even in a single blade of grass
the cool breeze
finds a home
— ISSA

The trout leaps up—
and below him in a stream
clouds float by
— ONITSURA

How quiet—
at the bottom of the lake
peaks of clouds

—Issa

At the sound of the sea
the sunflowers open
their black eyes

—Yūji

Octopus pot—
evanescent dreams
of the summer moon

—Bashō

Short summer night—
flowing through reeds
bubbles from crabs
— BUSON

Stillness—
seeping into the rocks
the cicada's voice
— BASHŌ

How beautifully
the cow has slimmed down
in the summer fields
— Bonchō

In the morning dew
soiled and cooled—
dirt on the melon
— Bashō

Summer coolness—
lantern out,
the sound of water

—SHIKI

Summer rains—
secretly one evening
moon in the pines

—RYŌTA

The bat's
secret home—
a tattered hat

—BUSON

Evening glories—
the cat chewing the flower
has its mind elsewhere

— BUSON

Among the ears of barley
are you hiding your tail?
old fox

— TESSHI

The coming of autumn
determined
　　by a red dragonfly
　　　　　—SHIRAO

The stars
have already opened
　　their autumn eyes
　　　　　—KŌYŌ

Early autumn—
the evening shower becomes
a night of rain

— TAIGI

Autumn begins—
ocean and fields
all one green

— BASHŌ

Early autumn—
peering through willows
the morning sun

— SEIBI

Morning glories—
blown to the ground
bloom as they are

—ISSA

As dew drips
gently, gently, the dove
murmurs its chant

—ISSA

Grasses and trees all
waiting for the moon—
dewy evening

—SŌGI

White dew
on brambles and thorns—
one drop each

— BUSON

On blades of grass
frolic and roll on—
pearls of dew

— RANSETSU

Dew cooling—
things with shapes
all alive

—KIJŌ

Its face
looks like a horse—
the grasshopper

—ANONYMOUS

Dragonfly on a rock
absorbed in
a daydream

—SANTŌKA

The dragonfly
cannot come to rest
on the blades of grass
—Bashō

Kittens
playing hide-and-seek
in the bush clover
—Issa

Dragonflies
quiet their mad darting—
crescent moon
—Kikaku

The bat
circling the moon
would not leave it

— Kyōtai

Give me back my dream!
a crow has wakened me
to misty moonlight

— Onitsura

Dyeing his body
autumn—
the dragonfly

— BAKUSUI

Distant mountains
reflecting in its eyes—
a dragonfly

— ISSA

A floating sandal—
an object of scorn
to the plovers

— ANONYMOUS

The pine wind
circling around the eaves—
autumn deepens

—BASHŌ

Cool breeze
filling the empty sky—
pine voices

—ONITSURA

To the mountain quietude
the quiet
rain

—SANTŌKA

The old dog
is leading the way—
    visiting family graves
                    —Issa

Typhoons ended,
the rat swims across
    flowing waters
                    —Buson

Calling three times,
then no more to be heard—
the deer in the rain
— BUSON

Running across the shelf
hoisting a chrysanthemum—
a temple mouse
— TAKAMASA

On a withered branch
lingers the evanescent memory
of a cicada's voice

— KAGAI

Singing as it goes,
an insect floats down the stream
on a broken bough

— ISSA

"The eyes of the hawks
are now dimmed,"
quails sing

— BASHŌ

A grasshopper
chirps in the sleeve
of the scarecrow
— CHIGETSU

The fields have withered—
no need for the crane
to stretch out its neck
— SHIKŌ

The first goose
seeking its own sky
in the dusk
— SHIRŌ

When they fall,
just as they fall—
garden grasses

— RYŌKAN

Mountains darken—
robbing the scarlet
from maple leaves

— BUSON

The moon speeds on—
the treetops
    still holding rain

—Bashō

A rock
against the moon
    sits big

—Seisensui

The bright moon—
out from the sleeve
   of the scarecrow

          —ISSA

Fallen leaves
fall on each other—
   rain beats on the rain

          —KYŌTAI

Blown from the west
collecting in the east—
   falling leaves

          —BUSON

The old pond's
frog also growing old—
fallen leaves

— BUSON

Sweeping
and then not sweeping
the fallen leaves

— TAIGI

Very squarely
setting its buttocks down—
the pumpkin

— SŌSEKI

The autumn wind
takes the shape
of pampas grass

— KIGIN

To passing autumn
the pampas grass waves
goodbye goodbye

— SHIRAO

Autumn rains—
a spider encased in
a clump of fallen grass
— SEKITEI

Evening fog—
my horse has learned
the holes on the bridge
— ISSA

The sound
of the raindrops
also grown older
— SANTŌKA

In the harvest moonlight
standing nonchalantly—
the scarecrow
— ISSA

Its hat fallen off
and embarrassed—
the scarecrow
— BUSON

A rinse of vermilion poured
from the setting sun, and then
autumn dusk

— Taigi

The bitter persimmons
spending their autumn
quietly

— Ritō

Garden gate
slamming and thwacking—
autumn wind

— Haritsu

Just like people
the monkey clasps its hands—
autumn wind

—SHADŌ

One edge
hanging over the mountain—
the Milky Way

—SHIKI

The moon in the water
turns somersaults
and flows away
— SANO RYŌTA

Whiter than
the stones of Stone Mountain—
the autumn wind
— BASHŌ

The autumn wind
at the sliding door—
a piercing voice
— BASHŌ

The huge setting sun—
little remains of
its power
— KYOSHI

All in calmness—
the earth with half-opened eyes
moves into winter
— DAKOTSU

New garden
stones settling down—
first winter rain

—Shadō

Red berries—
just one has fallen
frosty garden

—Shiki

Without a companion,
abandoned in the fields
winter moon

—Roseki

Camphor-tree roots
silently soak in
the early winter rain
— BUSON

How amusing,
it may change into snow—
the winter rain
— BASHŌ

Crescent moon warped
coldness
    keen and clear
                —Issa

First snow—
just enough to bend
    the narcissus leaves
                —Bashō

On the mandarin duck's wings
a dust of snow—
    such stillness!

— SHIKI

Cold moon—
the gateless temple's
    endless sky

— BUSON

Unable to wrap it
and dropping the moon—
    the winter rain

— TOKOKU

How warm—
the shadows of withered trees
stretching out their arms
—Tei-jo

There's nothing
he doesn't know—
the cat on the stove
—Fūsei

On a mandarin duck
its beauty is exhausted—
winter grove
—Buson

The sea grows dark
the voice of the duck
faintly whitens

— Bashō

Cold moon—
among the withered trees
three stalks of bamboo

— Buson

Its saddle taken off
how cold it looks—
the horse's rump
— Hekigodō

Snow
falls on snow—
and remains silent
— Santōka

Wolves
are keening in harmony—
snowy evening

—Jōsō

If it had no voice
the heron might disappear—
this morning's snow

—Chiyo-jo

Dawn—
the storm is buried
in snow

—Shirō

Withered by winter
one-colored world—
the sound of wind
— BASHŌ

The winter moon
trailing its white glow
leaves the mountain
— DAKOTSU

The salted sea bream's
teeth are also chilly—
fish-market shelf
— BASHŌ

Bleakly, bleakly
the sun enters into the rocks—
a withered field

— BUSON

Blistering wind—
splintered by rocks
the voice of the water

— BUSON

Today is also ending—
at the bottom of the snowstorm
a gigantic sun

—Arō

Wintry blasts—
blown off into the ocean
the evening sun

—Sōseki

Sad stories
whispered to the jellyfish
by the sea slug

— SHŌHA

Frozen together,
what are they dreaming?
sea slugs

— SEISEI

In the eyes of the hawk
over the withered fields
sits the winter storm

— JŌSŌ

Coming to the sea
the winter wind has no place
to return

— SEISHI

In the abandoned boat
dashing and sliding—
hail

— SHIKI

Flowing down
ice crushes
ice

— GOMEI

The winter storm
hides in the bamboo
and becomes silent
— BASHŌ

Dearly, dearly
embracing the sun—
the fallen garden leaves
— RITŌ

Each plum blossom
brings a single blossom's
warmth

— Bashō

The warbler
sings upside-down
his first note

— Kikaku

Human Voices

The tiny child—
shown even a flower
opens its mouth

—Seifu-jo

Flea bites—
while counting them, she nurses
her baby

—Issa

Shielding an infant
from the wind—
a scarecrow

—Issa

Garden butterfly—
as the baby crawls, it flies
crawls—flies—

— Issa

A child on my back
I picked a bracken shoot
and let him hold it

— Kyōtai

Her mother eats
the bitter parts—
    mountain persimmons

—Issa

The harvest moon—
"Get it for me!"
    cries the child

—Issa

"It's this big!"
forming a peony with her arms—
a child

—Issa

Today too!
today too! kites caught
by the nettle tree

—Issa

Spring rains—
a child teaches the cat
a dance

—Issa

Worse than tears—
the smile of the
abandoned child
— Anonymous

The season's first melon
clutched in its arms
sleeps the child
— Issa

Blazing sun—
whose barefoot child
is running free?
— Kōyō

At the ticket window
our child becomes
one year younger

— SEIUN

The youngest child
visiting family graves
carries the broom

— BUSON

First love—
coming close to a lantern
face-to-face
                    —Taigi

Secret night rendezvous—
a mosquito was swatted
and died quietly
                    —Anonymous

Heaven knows,
earth knows, every neighbor knows—
parents don't know
　　　　　—SHISHŌSHI

Sharing one umbrella—
the person more in love
gets wet
　　　　　—KEISANJIN

Catching up
and looking at her—
nothing special
　　　　　—ANONYMOUS

Hearing footsteps
splitting in two
the shadow
— Anonymous

Waving umbrellas
"goodbye" . . . "goodbye" . . .
gossamer haze
— Issa

Having children,
you understand—
but too late
— Anonymous

Pear blossoms—
a woman reads a letter
by moonlight

—BUSON

Harvesting radishes,
he points the way
with a radish

—ISSA

Workers—
they laugh
　　in a single color
　　　　　—HAKUSHI

Selling ladles,
he shows how to scoop up
　　nothing at all
　　　　　—ANONYMOUS

Chanting the Lotus Sutra—
only his lips
　　are busy
　　　　　—ANONYMOUS

With both hands
thrust up mightily—
my yawn

—ANONYMOUS

Trout fishing—
more fishermen
than trout

—KENJIN

Very secretly
the medicine peddler
is sick

—ANONYMOUS

The convalescent—
indulging in his mother's care
has become a habit
— Anonymous

Losing,
he straightens in his seat
and loses again
— Anonymous

Having given my opinion
I return home to
my wife's opinion
— Yachō

Priding himself
on scolding
his beautiful wife
— Anonymous

"Every woman . . ."
he starts to say,
then looks around
— ANONYMOUS

"After you die
they'll be valuable"
he tells the painter
— ANONYMOUS

Skeletons
covered with adornment—
flower viewing
— ONITSURA

Wanting to be logical
he tries so hard—
the drunkard
— Meitei

"Let's pull them all"
says the dentist
generously
— Anonymous

"I'd never lose
in a sumo match"—
pillow talk

— BUSON

No talents
also no sins—
winter seclusion

— ISSA

Winter seclusion—
from my wife and children
I too play hide-and-seek
— BUSON

New Year's cards
with women's handwriting
get looked at first
— BIRIKEN

She lowers
her eloquent lap
onto his silent lap
— ANONYMOUS

The kimono for flower-viewing—
disrobing, I'm entwined in
a myriad of sashes
—Hisa-jo

Without a word
the guest, the host,
white chrysanthemums
—Ryōta

Out from the gate,
I too become a traveler—
autumn dusk
—Buson

Walking along the river
with no bridge to cross—
the day is long

— SHIKI

Cold moon—
feeling the pebbles
under my shoes

— BUSON

A single guest
visits a single host—
autumn evening

— BUSON

"Coming, coming,"
but someone still knocks—
snowy gate

— KYORAI

My *go* rival—
how vexing
     and how dear
                    —Anonymous

Getting old—
I slip on a watermelon rind
     as I dance
                    —Sōchō

My nose running
I play a solitary *go*-game—
     night chill
                    —Buson

Just asking them to fight,
he saved tons of money
and died

—Hakuchō

Flesh getting thin—
these are thick bones

—Hōsai

Feeling my bones
on the quilting—
frosty night

— BUSON

Charcoal fire—
my years dwindle down
just like that

— ISSA

For me leaving
for you staying
    two autumns

— SHIKI

Owning nothing—
such peace,
    such coolness!

— ISSA

Left to live on
left to live on and on—
    this cold

— ISSA

Loneliness
also has its pleasure—
autumn dusk

—Buson

Autumn of my years—
the moon is perfect
and yet—

—Issa

Walking the dog
you meet
lots of dogs

—Sōshi

Taking a nap
I hide within myself—
    winter seclusion

— BUSON

All of a sudden
my first fallen tooth—
    autumn wind

— SANPŪ

Winter rain—
I'm not dead yet
                    — SANTŌKA

A whole family
all gray-haired with canes
     visits graves
                    — BASHŌ

This autumn
no child in my lap—
moon-viewing
— ONITSURA

Are my youthful dreams
still unfinished?
this morning's frost
— ANONYMOUS

The auspiciousness
is just about medium—
my spring
— ISSA

On New Year's Day
the morning in town
comes irregularly
— ANONYMOUS

First winter kimono—
may you quickly grow to
a naughty age
— ISSA

Snow has melted—
the village is full
of children
— ISSA

Resonance and Reverberation

"Don't dare break it!"
but he broke off and gave me
a branch of garden plum

— TAIGI

Spring river—
a tiny wooden clog
floats by

— HARITSU

Spring rain—
blown onto the bush
a discarded letter

— ISSA

A shame to pick it
a shame to leave it—
　　the violet

　　　　　　　—Nao-jo

Even when chased
it pretends not to hurry—
　　the butterfly

　　　　　　　—Garaku

One sneeze—
and I lost sight of
the skylark

— YAYŪ

Tired heart—
mountains and ocean
too much beauty

— SANTŌKA

Lead him slowly!
the horse is carrying
the spring moon
— WATSUJIN

Come out!
you can almost touch
the spring moon
— TEI-JO

Spring moon—
if I touch it, it would
drip
— ISSA

Spring rain—
I gave my yawn
    to the dog at the gate
        —Issa

While I ponder
a snail
    passes me by
        —Anonymous

Frogs grow silent—
noble humans
    are passing by
        —Rakukyo

Early summer rain—
a letter from home
arrives wet
— HARITSU

Sudden shower—
riding naked
on a naked horse
— SANTŌKA

Rocks and trees
glisten in my eyes—
such heat

—KYORAI

The stone-carver
cools his chisel
in the clear stream

—BUSON

A hoe standing
with no one around—
the heat!

—SHIKI

Becoming a cow
would be fine—morning naps
and the evening cool
—Shikō

After my sneeze
all is quiet—
summer mountains
—Yasui

Only the moon and I
remain on the bridge
    cooling off
                — KIKUSHA

One person
and one fly
    in the large room
                — ISSA

The fly on the porch
while rubbing its hands—
    swat!
                — ISSA

Each time
I swat a fly, I chant
"Namu Amida Butsu"
— Issa

Mosquito larvae,
dancing a Buddhist chant
in the water by the grave
— Issa

Being hit
the gong spits out
a noontime mosquito
— Sōseki

Sharing the same blood
but we're not related—
    the hateful mosquito!
            —Jōsō

The flute player
bitten by a mosquito
    on the edge of his lips
            —Kyoriku

Swarms of mosquitoes—
but without them,
    it's a little lonely

— Issa

During the day
the Buddha shelters behind
    mosquitoes

— Issa

The beggar
wears heaven and earth
as summer clothes
— KIKAKU

Where there are people
there are flies, and
there are Buddhas
— ISSA

They live long—
the flies, fleas, and mosquitoes
in this poor village
— ISSA

Two old bent backs
sitting close, wrapped in
    a shower of cicada songs
        — Anonymous

In my hand
its fleeting light vanishes—
    the firefly

        — Kyorai

How delightful
walking on dewy grasses—
straw sandals
— HARITSU

Killing the spider
then so lonesome—
evening cold
— SHIKI

Seeing that I'm old
even the mosquito whispers
closer to my ear

— Issa

An autumn mosquito
determined to die
bites me

— Shiki

Before the white mums
hesitating for a while—
the scissors

— Buson

Truly the autumn has come—
I was convinced
by my sneeze
— BUSON

Planting my buttocks
on a huge taro leaf—
moon-viewing
— HARITSU

Whatever they wear
they become beautiful
moon-viewing
— CHIYO-JO

Taking me along
my shadow comes home
from moon-viewing

—Sodō

Even grandma
goes out drinking—
moonlit night

—Issa

Wild geese muttering, muttering—
are they spreading
   rumors about me?

        — Issa

Don't cry, wild geese,
it's the same everywhere—
   this floating world

        — Issa

A man raking—
the leaves keep
   calling him back

        — Anonymous

Dusk—
while the earth and I talk
     leaves fall

— Issa

When I show my delight
they fall down faster—
     acorns

— Fūsei

Coldly, coldly
the sun slips into my sleeve—
     autumn mountains

— Issa

Autumn wind—
in my heart, how many
mountains and rivers
— KYOSHI

Deep in the mountains—
falling into my heart
autumn streams
— SHINKEI

More than last year
it is lonely—
 the autumn dusk
— BUSON

On my shoulder
is it longing for a companion?
 a red dragonfly
— SŌSEKI

Love in my old age—
as I try to forget,
late autumn rain

— Buson

When I finally die—
weeds
falling rain

— Santōka

From the nose
of the Buddha in the fields—
icicles

— Issa

Visitors
kindly create a path
through the snow at my gate
—Issa

The black dog
becomes a lantern—
snowy road
—Anonymous

Winter sun—
frozen on horseback
is my shadow
—Bashō

Piercing cold—
I dropped my broom
under the pines

— TAIGI

Colder than snow
on my white hair—
the winter moon

— JŌSŌ

A hundred miles of frost—
in a boat, I own
the moon
— BUSON

Peaceful, peaceful
chilly, chilly
snow, snow
— SANTŌKA

To my cat
a New Year's card
from its vet

—Yorie

The child on my lap
begins to point at
plum blossoms

—Issa

Plum blossoms—
"Steal this one here!"
points the moon

—Issa

Under the trees
into the salad, into the soup—
cherry blossoms

            —Bashō

THE POETS

ARŌ. See **USUDA ARŌ**.

BAISHITSU (1769–1852). Baishitsu was born in Kanazawa to a family of sword experts. He moved to Kyoto, visited Edo (Tokyo) for twelve years, and then settled again in Kyoto, where he became one of the major haiku teachers of his era.

BAKUSUI (1718–83). A poet from Kanazawa during the middle of the Edo Period, Bakusui studied under Otsuyū.

BASHŌ (1644–94). Widely admired as the greatest of all haiku masters, Bashō, when young, left samurai life when his lord passed away and devoted himself to poetry. He made several journeys, which he celebrated in combinations of prose and haiku called *haibun,* and his deep humanity and depth of spirit influenced Japanese literature profoundly.

BIRIKEN (dates and details unknown).

BONCHŌ (died 1714). By profession a doctor, Bonchō edited a famous book of haiku poems with Kyorai, and also wrote many fresh and original haiku of his own. He was also interested in European studies, and was imprisoned for trading illegally with Dutch merchants.

BŌSAI. See **KAMEDA BŌSAI**.

BUSON (1716–83). Around the age of seventeen, Buson went to Edo (Tokyo) and studied painting and haiku. After his haiku teacher's death in 1742, Buson wandered around the eastern provinces for more than ten years, later settling in Kyoto. Buson is now considered one of the greatest artists in the literati style, and second only to Bashō in the haiku tradition. Buson's verses as well as his paintings show the warmth and brilliance of his vision of humanity and the natural world.

CHIGETSU (1634?–1708?). Chigetsu, the wife of a freight agent, studied haiku with Bashō, and became one of the four famous women poets of her era. After the death of her husband in 1686, she became a nun. She lived in Ōtsu with her son, Otokuni, who also studied with Bashō and became a fine haiku poet.

CHINE-JO (?–1688?). Chine-jo was the younger sister of Kyorai, who was one of the ten leading pupils of Bashō. In her early twenties, Chine-jo and Kyorai traveled together to Ise. During this trip, Chine-jo wrote haiku poems that were considered as good as or even better than those by her elder brother.

CHIYO-JO (1703–75). Beginning to write haiku on her own at the age of fifteen, Chiyo-jo later studied with Shikō and eventually became a nun. Her haiku style achieved great popularity with its direct expression and witty mastery of language.

CHORA (1719–80). Born in Shima (present-day Mie Prefecture), Chora later moved to Ise. He associated with poets such as Buson.

CHŌSUI (1701–69). A poet in the middle of the Edo Period, Chōsui was born the son of a local governor in Chiba, and he later became a monk. One of his haiku disciples was Shirao.

DAKOTSU. See **IIDA DAKOTSU**.

EIJI (dates and details unknown).

FUKUDA HARITSU (1865–1944). Born in the small town of Shingū in Wakayama Prefecture, Fukuda Haritsu became a pupil of Shiki in Tokyo, then moved to Kyoto where he led the life of a scholar-poet using the name Kodōjin (Old Taoist). He wrote haiku, *waka,* and Chinese-style poetry, and painted both *haiga* and literati landscapes.

FŪSEI. See **TOMIYASU FŪSEI**.

GARAKU (dates and details unknown).

GIBON. See **SENGAI GIBON**.

GOMEI (1731–1803). A poet in Akita Prefecture, Gomei studied Bashō's haiku on his own.

HAKUCHŌ (dates and details unknown).

HAKUSHI (dates unknown). A writer of humorous verse from Edo (Tokyo).

HARA SEKITEI (1886–1951). Born in Shimane Prefecture, Sekitei studied under Takahama Kyoshi. He was active in the haiku journal *Hototogisu* and he was also skilled in *haiga* painting.

HARITSU. See FUKUDA HARITSU.

HEKIGODŌ. See KAWAHIGASHI HEKIGODŌ.

HISA-JO. See SUGITA HISA-JO.

HŌITSU (1761–1828). Born in Edo (Tokyo) to the Sakai family, lord of Himeji fiefdom, Hōitsu excelled as a haiku poet and also a painter in the decorative tradition.

HŌSAI. See OZAKI HŌSAI.

IIDA DAKOTSU (1885–1962). Born in Yamanashi Prefecture, Dakotsu studied at Waseda University. He was one of the representative poets of the haiku journal *Hototogisu*.

ISSA (1763–1827). A poet whose life was filled with personal tragedy, Issa became the most compassionate of all haiku masters, with a special feeling for children and common people.

Jōsō (1662–1704). Due to poor health, Jōsō gave up his samurai position at the age of twenty-six and became a monk. He studied haiku with Bashō, and after the death of his master lived a quiet and solitary life.

Kagai (died 1778, details unknown).

Kaiga (1652–1718). A pupil of Bashō, Kaiga was a close friend of the poet Kikaku.

Kameda Bōsai (1752–1826). One of the leading Confucian scholars and Chinese-style poet-calligraphers of his day, Bōsai only rarely wrote haiku. He inscribed his verse about "the old pond" over a portrait of Bashō.

Kana-jo (dates unknown). A Kyoto poet, Kana-jo was Kyorai's wife and had two daughters.

Kansetsu (dates and details unknown).

Kawahigashi Hekigodō (1873–1937). Born in Matsuyama, Ehime Prefecture, Hekigodō studied with Shiki. He also wrote literary criticism and novels.

Keisanjin (dates and details unknown).

Kenjin (dates and details unknown).

Kichō (dates unknown). Kichō was best known as a critic and evaluator of poetry competitions during the Edo Period.

Kigin (1624–1705). Born in Shiga Prefecture, Kigin

was known as a scholar of classics. He served the *bakufu* government. Kigin learned haiku with Teitoku, whose pupils included Bashō.

Kijō. See **Murakami Kijō**.

Kikaku (1661–1707). One of the ten leading pupils of Bashō, Kikaku was also an expert in Chinese-style poetry, Confucianism, medicine, calligraphy, and painting. His poetic style is known for its wit and humor.

Kikusha (1753–1826). Born in Yamaguchi, Kikusha devoted herself to the arts, including painting, calligraphy, *waka*, Chinese-style verse, and haiku. After her husband died when she was twenty-four years old, she became a nun.

Kinoshita Yūji (1914–65). Born in Hiroshima Prefecture, Yūji took over his father's pharmacy store. As a poet, he was recognized by Kubota Mantarō, a popular literary figure of the time.

Kitō (1741–89). Learning haiku first from his father and later from Buson, Kitō also greatly admired the poems of Kikaku. Kitō wrote haiku with direct and unsentimental observations. He loved *sake,* and like several other haiku poets he became a monk in his final years.

Kōji (dates and details unknown).

Kōyō. See **Ozaki Kōyō**.

KUBOTA MANTARŌ (1889–1963). Mantarō was born in Asakusa, Tokyo. After graduating from Keiō University, he became famous as a writer, dramatist, and also a stage producer. Mantarō's poems are characterized by their lyrical quality.

KUBO YORIE (1884–1967). Born in Matsuyama, Yorie met Shiki and Sōseki when she was young and became interested in haiku.

KYORAI (1651–1704). Born in Nagasaki, Kyorai moved to Kyoto at the age of eight and became known for his excellence in martial arts, astronomy, and general learning. He met Kikaku in 1684 and joined him to become one of the ten leading pupils of Bashō. He combined in his own verse the qualities of martial strength and poetic gentleness. Kyorai's writings about poetics became influential for later haiku masters.

KYORIKU (1656–1715). A samurai in the Hikone region (present-day Shiga Prefecture), Kyoriku excelled in the lance, sword, and horseback riding. He was also a good painter in the Kanō style. He studied haiku with Bashō.

KYOSHI. See **TAKAHAMA KYOSHI**.

KYŌTAI (1732–92). A native of Nagoya, Kyōtai tried to elevate haiku from the vulgarity of his day and return to the excellence of Bashō. He also followed the lead of Buson in creating poems combining strength of imagery with keen observation of the world around him.

MANTARŌ. See **KUBOTA MANTARŌ**.

MASAOKA SHIKI (1867–1902). Despite the brevity of his life, Shiki became the most influential haiku poet and theorist of the late nineteenth century. He insisted that haiku poets should cultivate the keen observation (*shasei*) of nature. He established the famous haiku journal *Hototogisu*.

MATSUSE SEISEI (1869–1937). A poet from Osaka, Seisei was a follower of Shiki and wrote haiku in traditional style, opposing radical change in the world of poetry. In 1902, he became the haiku editor of *The Asahi* newspaper.

MEITEI. See **TSUKAKOSHI MEITEI**.

MIZUOCHI ROSEKI (1872–1919). Born in Osaka, Mizuochi Roseki studied haiku with Shiki. He was considered to be the leader of the Osaka haiku group of the time.

MURAKAMI KIJŌ (1865–1938). Born as the eldest son of a low-ranking samurai in Tottori, Kijō suffered from constant poverty. He was an early representative of the haiku journal *Hototogisu*.

NAKAMURA TEI-JO (1900–1988). Born in Kumamoto, Tei-jo joined the haiku journal *Hototogisu*.

She promoted women's haiku writing through mass media.

Nao-jo (dates and details unknown).

Natsume Sōseki (1867–1916). The most famous novelist of his time, Sōseki studied in England and later taught English literature in Japan. Less known as a haiku poet, he nevertheless wrote many fine verses.

Ogiwara Seisensui (1884–1976). Born in Tokyo, Seisensui graduated from Tokyo University, majoring in linguistics. He advocated free-style haiku. Taneda Santōka was one of his followers. He wrote widely on Issa and Bashō.

Okada Yachō (1882–1960). Born in Tsuyama City, Yachō started composing *senryū* in his early twenties. He engaged in farming and was a gentle person known for *senryū* with topics taken from his daily life.

Onitsura (1661–1738). At the age of eight, Onitsura began to learn haiku. At thirteen, he became a pupil of Matsue Shigeyori, and he also received instructions from Kitamura Kigin and Nishiyama Sōin. In 1865, Onitsura stated that he came to realize that sincerity was the most important quality in poetry. Thus, his haiku poems were written in a simple and straightforward style.

Ontei. See **Shinohara Ontei**.

Otsuyū (1675–1739). Also known as Bakurin, Otsuyū was a priest at Ise. He studied with Bashō when Bashō visited his area. He also painted *haiga*.

Ozaki Hōsai (1885–1926). Spending his life working at temples, Ozaki Hōsai wrote haiku noted for their free form and direct language.

Ozaki Kōyō (1867–1903). Known primarily for his novels such as *Golden Demon*, written in colloquial style, Kōyō was also a fine haiku poet during his short life.

Raizan (1654–1716). A merchant in Osaka, Raizan started with comical and witty haiku but later changed to a more serious style close to Bashō's.

Rakukyo (dates and details unknown).

Rankō (1726–98). Born in Kanazawa, Ronkō later moved to Kyoto, where he practiced medicine. He promoted Bashō's haiku style by compiling the master's writings.

Ransetsu (1654–1707). Ransetsu studied painting with Hanabusa Itchō, a famous painter, and haiku under Bashō. Ransetsu also studied Zen Buddhism, and its influence is discernible in his later haiku. He was one of the disciples whom Master Bashō highly appreciated, and is known for his gentle and sophisticated poetic style.

Ritō (1681–1755). An Edo poet, Ritō was one of the pupils of Ransetsu. One of his followers was Ryōta.

Roseki. See **Mizuochi Roseki**.

Ryōkan (1758–1831). Born in Echigo, present-day Niigata Prefecture, Ryōkan became a Zen monk. He spent his life, full of interesting episodes (some of which are legendary), in poverty as an itinerant monk. His poems are full of a wonderful free spirit. Ryōkan also excelled in *waka* poetry, Chinese poetry, and calligraphy.

Ryōta (1718–87). When young, Ryōta moved to Edo (Tokyo) and studied with Ritō, Ransetsu's pupil. He then became a haiku teacher and was reported to have many pupils under him.

Saimaro (1656–1738). Born to a samurai household, Saimaro studied haiku with Ihara Saikaku, the famous fiction writer and haiku poet of the time. Saimaro also kept an association with Bashō. Later in his life, he enjoyed considerable power in the Osaka haiku world.

Sano Ryōta (1890–1954). Born in Niigata Prefecture, Ryōta was known for his fresh expressions of nature.

Sanpū (1647–1732). A pupil and patron of Bashō, Sanpū provided the master with his famous cottage Bashō-an (Banana Plant Hermitage).

Santōka. See **Taneda Santōka**.

Seibi (1749–1816). Born into a wealthy family, Seibi associated with Shirao and Kyōtai. He was known as one of the three great haiku poets of his day along with Michihiko and Sōchō. He was Issa's benefactor.

Seifu-jo (1731–1814). Born in Musashi Province, Seifu-jo studied with Chōsui and Shirao. Her haiku style is often highly subjective and personal.

Seisei. See **Matsuse Seisei**.

Seisensui. See **Ogiwara Seisensui**.

Seishi. See **Yamaguchi Seishi**.

Seiun (dates and details unknown).

Sekitei. See **Hara Sekitei**.

Sengai Gibon (1750–1837). A Zen master from Kyushu, Sengai became beloved for his paintings, which often show his delightful sense of humor.

Shadō (died 1737?). A poet and doctor in Ōmi (present-day Shiga Prefecture) area, Shadō studied haiku under Bashō and participated in Bashō's haiku-composing gatherings. He published one of Bashō's well-known anthologies, *Hisago* (Gourd).

Shigeyori (1602–80). Born in Matsue, Shigeyori lived most of his life in Kyoto. He studied haiku with Teitoku. He later compiled Bashō's haiku, and had fine haiku pupils such as Onitsura.

SHIKI. See **MASAOKA SHIKI**.

SHIKŌ (1665–1731). After serving as a Zen monk at Daichi-ji, Shikō became a doctor, later meeting and becoming a disciple of Bashō. When told he might be reborn as an animal if he did not lead a pure life, Shikō observed that it might well be an improvement.

SHINKEI (1406–75). A linked-verse (*renga*) poet, Shinkei was an influential figure for the next generation of the linked-verse poets, such as Sōgi.

SHINOHARA ONTEI (1872–1926). Born in Kumamoto Prefecture, Ontei worked for a newspaper company in Tokyo and studied haiku under Shiki and Kyoshi.

SHIRAO (1738–91). Born in Shinano (present-day Nagano Prefecture) and studying haiku in Edo (Tokyo), Shirao later traveled to many areas and vigorously taught haiku. He wrote several manuscripts on haiku theory that emphasized naturalness of expression.

SHIRŌ (1742–1812). Born in Nagoya, Shirō practiced medicine. He studied haiku with Kyōtai and was also known for his skill in playing the *biwa* (lute).

SHISHŌSHI (1866–1928). Born in Tokyo, Shishōshi was very active in promoting *senryū* and mentored many poets.

SHŌHA (died 1771). Shōha studied Chinese poems

with Hattori`Nankaku. A beloved haiku pupil of
Buson, Shōha died before his teacher, and Buson
thereupon wrote a preface for Shōha's collected haiku
that became very famous. Shōha's own poems show
his keen visual sense.

SHOKYŪ (1741–81). Born in Echigo (present-day Nii-
gata Prefecture), Shokyū took the tonsure after her
husband's death. She also traveled widely.

SHŪSHIKI-JO (1669–1725?). Shūshiki-jo studied with
Kikaku, and she married the haiku poet Kangyoku,
also a pupil of Kikaku. Shūshiki-jo's poems became
famous for their gentle and humane observations of
everyday life.

SŌCHŌ (1761–1814). The son of the famous calligra-
pher Yamamoto Ryōsai, Sōchō became a successful
artist and haiku poet in Edo (Tokyo).

SODŌ (1642–1716). Born in Kai, Sodō moved to Edo
(Tokyo) and became associated with Bashō.

SŌGI (1421–1502). A highly respected linked-verse
(*renga*) master and literary theorist, Sōgi excelled in
calligraphy. He was also very well learned in classical
poetry, and he lectured to many nobles and high of-
ficials, including a shogun. Sōgi's linked-verse collec-
tion *Minase Sangin Hyakuin* (One Hundred Verses by
Three Poets at Minase), which he composed with two
other masters, represents a high point of linked verse.

Sōkan (1458?–1546?). From a samurai family, Sōkan served the shogun Ashikaga Yoshihisa. After his father's death, however, Sōkan became a monk and lived the rest of his life in a hermitage, where he developed a new form of simplified linked-verse (*renga*) poetry. In time he became considered the inventor of haiku.

Sora (1649–1710). Giving up his life as a samurai, Sora went to Edo (Tokyo) and studied Shintō and *waka* with Kikkawa Koretaru. Later, Sora became a pupil of Bashō and often traveled with his teacher on haiku journeys.

Sōseki. See **Natsume Sōseki**.

Sōshi (dates and details unknown).

Sugita Hisa-jo (1890–1946). A poet in the coterie of Takahama Kyoshi, Sugita Hisa-jo married a painter. Her haiku style has a rich romantic flavor.

Taigi (1709–71). Born in Edo (Tokyo), Taigi moved to the entertainment district of Kyoto, where he became associated with Buson. He is known for his haiku on human affairs.

Takahama Kyoshi (1874–1959). Kyoshi was one of the masters of the haiku tradition in the late Meiji, Taishō, and early Shōwa periods. The name Kyoshi was given him by Masaoka Shiki. Kyoshi inherited Shiki's haiku magazine *Hototogisu* and continued Shiki's literary circle, where writers and poets reviewed their own works. Kyoshi also wrote novels and essays, but was most celebrated for his poems, which were traditional in style but fresh in spirit.

TAKAMASA (late seventeenth to early eighteenth century). A follower of the Kyoto Danrin school of haiku, Takamasa lived in Kyoto and befriended pupils of Teitoku. He wrote haiku poems describing natural scenes in an unpretentious, free, and sometimes wild style.

TANEDA SANTŌKA (1882–1940). Born in Yamaguchi Prefecture, he attended Waseda University but never graduated. He studied haiku under Seisensui. After the bankruptcy of his household, he divorced his wife and became a monk. He spent his life as a traveling monk composing free-style haiku.

TEI-JO. See **NAKAMURA TEI-JO**.

TEISHITSU (1610–73). Running a paper business in Kyoto, Teishitsu studied haiku under Teitoku. He was also a skilled musician, playing the *biwa* (lute) and flute.

TESSHI (died 1707). Tesshi traveled widely in the Kansai, Kantō, and northern areas of Japan. The book by Tesshi entitled *Hanamiguruma* is a collection of gossip about haiku poets, who appear in the book as courtesans.

TOKOKU (?–1690). A rice merchant in Nagoya, Tokoku became Bashō's pupil when the latter came to the area. He traveled with Bashō, and his death was deeply lamented by his master.

TOMIYASU FŪSEI (1885–1979). Fūsei traveled in Europe and the United States, then returned to Japan to study under Kyoshi. Eventually he became one of the leading haiku poets of the twentieth century.

TSUKAKOSHI MEITEI (1894–1965). A poet born in Tokyo, Meitei worked for newspaper companies, one of which was in Taiwan. He created a Taiwan *senryū* circle before returning to Japan after World War II.

USUDA ARŌ (1879–1951). Born in Nagano Prefecture, Arō learned haiku under Takahama Kyoshi.

WATSUJIN (1758–1836). A poet in the Kyōtai tradition, Watsujin was a samurai from Sendai who wrote haiku under a variety of art names.

YACHŌ. See **OKADA YACHŌ**.

YAMAGUCHI SEISHI (1901–94). Born in Kyoto, he was a member of the haiku journal *Hototogisu*. He introduced new ideas to haiku through his poems.

YASUI (1658–1743). A merchant from Nagoya, Yasui wrote many haiku following the Bashō tradition. Later in his life, Yasui shifted his interest to *waka* and the tea ceremony.

YAYŪ (1702–83). Yayūwas a retainer of the Owari family, one of the three branch families of the Tokugawa clan. After he retired, Yayū spent his life creating haiku and paintings. He was also known for his *haibun* (poetic writing).

YORIE. See **KUBO YORIE**.

Yūji. See **KINOSHITA YŪJI**.

THE ARTISTS

HAKUIN EKAKU (1685–1768). Considered the most important Zen master of the past five hundred years, Hakuin was also the leading Zen painter, creating a large number of works with power, humor, and Zen intensity.

IKE TAIGA (1723–76). One of the great literati painters of Japan, Taiga was unusual in that he displayed his art fully at a youthful age, creating delightful transformations of the scholar-artist landscape painting tradition.

KI BAITEI (1734–1810). One of the major pupils of poet-painter Buson, Baitei (also known as Kyūrō) lived in Shiga Prefecture and created both landscapes and humorous figure studies.

MARUYAMA ŌKYO (1733–95). By creating a style that combined naturalism with influences from China and the West, Ōkyo became founder of the popular Maruyama school of painting.

MATSUYA JICHŌSAI (active 1781–88, died 1803?). Also known as Nichōsai, he was a sake brewer and antique dealer in Osaka who dabbled in poetry, painting, and singing. His humorous paintings have a caricature style all their own.

SESSON SHŪKEI (1504?–1589?). One of the major ink-painters of the late medieval period in Japan, Sesson was known for his strong compositions and bold brushwork.

TACHIBANA MORIKUNI (1679–1748). Born in Osaka, Morikuni studied the official style of the Kanō school, but was expelled because in one of his books he published designs that were considered secrets in the Kanō tradition.

YAMAGUCHI SOKEN (1759–1818). A pupil of the naturalistic master Ōkyo, Soken was especially gifted in his depictions of figure subjects.

THE ILLUSTRATIONS

SHAMBHALA LIBRARY

I Ching: The Book of Change, by Cheng Yi.
Translated by Thomas Cleary.

Love Poems from the Japanese, translated by Kenneth
Rexroth. Edited by Sam Hamill.

Lovingkindness: The Revolutionary Art of Happiness,
by Sharon Salzberg.

Mastering the Art of War, by Zhuge Liang and Liu Ji.
Translated by Thomas Cleary.

Meditation in Action, by Chögyam Trungpa.

The Myth of Freedom and the Way of Meditation,
by Chögyam Trungpa.

Nature and Other Writings, by Ralph Waldo
Emerson. Edited by Peter Turner.

New Seeds of Contemplation, by Thomas Merton.

No Man Is an Island, by Thomas Merton.

The Places That Scare You, by Pema Chödrön.

The Poetry of Zen, translated and edited by
Sam Hamill and J. P. Seaton.

*The Rumi Collection: An Anthology of Translations of
Mevlâna Jalâluddin Rumi.* Edited by Kabir Helminski.

The Sabbath: Its Meaning for Modern Man,
by Abraham Joshua Heschel.

Sailing Alone around the World,
by Captain Joshua Slocum.

Shambhala: The Sacred Path of the Warrior, by
Chögyam Trungpa. Edited by Carolyn Rose Gimian.

Siddhartha: A New Translation, by Hermann Hesse.
Translated by Sherab Chödzin Kohn.

*Start Where You Are: A Guide to Compassionate
Living,* by Pema Chödrön.

Tao Teh Ching, by Lao Tzu.
Translated by John C. H. Wu.

Teachings of the Buddha, edited by Jack Kornfield.

*The Tibetan Book of the Dead: The Great Liberation
through Hearing in the Bardo,* translated with
commentary by Francesca Fremantle
and Chögyam Trungpa.

Training the Mind and Cultivating Loving-Kindness,
by Chögyam Trungpa.

Walden, by Henry David Thoreau.
Illustrations by Michael McCurdy.

The Way of Chuang Tzu, by Thomas Merton.

The Way of the Bodhisattva, by Shantideva.
Translated by the Padmakara Translation Group.

*When Things Fall Apart: Heart Advice
for Difficult Times,* by Pema Chödrön.

The Wisdom of the Desert: Sayings from the Desert Fathers of the Fourth Century, by Thomas Merton.

The Wisdom of No Escape and the Path of Loving-Kindness, by Pema Chödrön.

Writing Down the Bones: Freeing the Writer Within, by Natalie Goldberg.

Zen Mind, Beginner's Mind, by Shunryu Suzuki.